C. 2

# Paul Revere

## History Maker Bios

## Jane Sutcliffe

LERNER PUBLICATIONS COMPANY • MINNEAPOLIS

*For my dad, Chester McCormick, who always had time to take me to the library*

Map on p. 29 by Laura Westlund
Illustrations by Tim Parlin

Text copyright © 2002 by Jane Sutcliffe
Illustrations copyright © 2002 by Lerner Publications Company

Lerner Publications Company
A division of Lerner Publishing Group
241 First Avenue North
Minneapolis, MN 55401 U.S.A.

Website address: www.lernerbooks.com


Library of Congress Cataloging-in-Publication Data

Sutcliffe, Jane.
     Paul Revere / by Jane Sutcliffe.
       p.    cm. — (History maker bios)
     Includes bibliographical references and index.
     ISBN: 0–8225–0195–3 (lib. bdg. : alk. paper)
       1. Revere, Paul, 1735–1818—Juvenile literature. 2. Statesmen—
     Massachusetts—Biography—Juvenile literature. 3. Massachusetts—
     Biography—Juvenile literature. 4. Massachusetts—History—Revolution,
     1775–1783—Juvenile literature. [1. Revere, Paul, 1735–1818. 2. Statesmen.
     3. Massachusetts—History—Revolution, 1775–1783—Biography. 4. United
     States—History—Revolution, 1775–1783—Biography.] I. Title. II. Series.
     F69.R43 S88 2002
     974.4'03'092—dc21                                              2001003272

Manufactured in the United States of America
1  2  3  4  5  6  –  JR  –  07  06  05  04  03  02

# Table of Contents

# INTRODUCTION

**M**ost Americans have heard about
Paul Revere's midnight ride. On
an April night in 1775, he galloped through
the Massachusetts countryside. He banged
on doors and shouted that British soldiers
were coming. His warning helped prepare
Americans for the start of the Revolutionary
War.

But Paul Revere was more than just a
noisy messenger on horseback. He was also
a father, a talented silversmith, and a
maker of many things. Most of all, he
worked hard to make the United States of
America an independent country.

This is his story.

# 1 BOSTON

**P**aul Revere was born in the winter of 1734, in Boston. When Paul was a boy, Boston was the busy capital of Massachusetts Bay, a colony of Great Britain.

Like most colonies in America, Massachusetts was ruled by the king of Britain and a group of British lawmakers called Parliament.

Boston was just the right kind of town for Paul Revere. Ships came and went in the crowded harbor. The crooked streets were a hubbub of pigs, dogs, and people. There were wharves, warehouses, and shops for Paul to explore. The city never seemed to rest and neither did Paul. He wanted to see and do everything.

At thirteen, Paul left school and began working in his father's shop. Mr. Revere was a silversmith. As his father's oldest son, Paul would be a silversmith, too.

*In Paul's day, Boston was one of the largest cities in the colonies.*

Paul had too much energy for just one job. When he was fifteen, he and his friends started a bell-ringers' club at nearby Christ Church. The church's steeple was so high, it could be seen clear across the Charles River from Charlestown. The church also had the sweetest-sounding bells.

The church bells did more than call people to church on Sunday. They were a way of spreading news.

Paul learned to turn silver coins into buttons, buckles, and spoons in his father's shop.

*Christ Church was one of the oldest churches in Boston. It later became known as Old North Church.*

Paul and his friends rang the bells that told people when a ship arrived in the harbor, or when the British Parliament passed a new law. It was an important job.

Not everyone was happy with the news that came from Britain. Most colonists thought of themselves as British. But some of them were disappointed with the way Britain treated the colonies. They thought the colonies should be allowed to make decisions for themselves.

Paul was so proud of his work as a silversmith that he chose to be painted with a teapot and some of his tools.

Other people, like Paul's father, were loyal to the king. Mr. Revere told Paul not to listen to such talk against Britain. Still, Paul was interested in hearing what people had to say—good or bad.

In 1754, when Paul was nineteen, his father died. Paul took over the silversmith shop. By now, Paul was a young man. He was not tall, but he was strong and sturdy. His warm, dark eyes were full of confidence.

In the summer of 1757, Paul married Sarah Orne. He and his new wife began filling their house with babies. They had eight in all.

The Revere house never seemed quite large enough for such a big family. But Paul didn't mind. He liked being surrounded by his children. He called them his little lambs.

To support his family, Paul worked hard in his silversmith shop. His customers demanded the very latest fashion in silver. Paul was talented at copying the styles from London.

## COLONIAL DENTIST

One way Paul made extra money was to be a dentist. It was his least favorite job. He cleaned people's teeth and made false teeth out of hippopotamus tusks. Making false teeth was a much-needed skill in colonial America. Most people's teeth were quite rotten. Sometimes even teenagers were missing half their teeth!

Paul designed teapots and sugar bowls with elegant shapes and graceful handles. By the time he was thirty, he was known as one of the finest silversmiths in Boston.

Sometimes Paul's work as a silversmith was not enough to pay the bills. He had to look for new ways to make money. That was fine with Paul. He was always happy to try something new. So he learned how to print business cards and hymnbooks. Paul also taught himself to make picture frames, clock faces, and spectacles.

Paul seemed to have the energy of two men. The people of Boston began to notice: Paul Revere was a man who knew how to get things done.

# 2 A SON OF LIBERTY

**E**ach evening, Paul snuffed out his candles and locked his shop. Then he often gathered with other men of Boston to discuss the news of the day. They met at taverns with names such as the Green Dragon and the Salutation.

Some of the men at these meetings were craftsmen like Paul. Others were rich men with college educations. More than anyone else in Boston, Paul was comfortable in both groups. People respected him.

There was much for Paul and his friends to discuss. The king and Parliament were demanding that the colonists pay more taxes. In the spring of 1765, Parliament passed a law called the Stamp Act. It meant that every contract Paul signed, and even the playing cards he used, had to have a special stamp.

The Green Dragon Tavern in Boston was a popular place to eat, drink, and complain about the British.

The stamp cost money. And of course, the money went straight to Britain. When Parliament was done with this tax, it ordered new ones on glass, paint, paper, and tea.

*All over the colonies, people met to discuss taxes.*

In taverns throughout Boston, fists were pounded on tables. After all, Paul and his friends said, the colonists were not allowed to vote for the lawmakers in Britain who were taxing them. That's what they meant when they said "No taxation without representation!" Angry colonists thought they should have more rights, and they said so.

Paul engraved this cartoon. It shows the king and his men making plans to take freedom away from the colonies.

Paul and his patriot friends wanted to do something to fight the unfair taxes. They formed a new group called the Sons of Liberty. Joseph Warren, Samuel Adams, and John Hancock were its leaders.

Some of the Sons wrote clever newspaper articles against the taxes. Paul fought in his own way. He engraved and printed political cartoons making fun of Britain. Paul was never as good at drawing as he was at making things from silver. Still, he got his point across.

By the fall of 1768, Britain had lost patience with the protests against taxes. The king sent soldiers marching into Boston. He hoped the sight of so many British soldiers would frighten the people of Boston into behaving.

The people didn't frighten so easily, though. Instead, they gave the soldiers a hard time. Young boys called them lobsters or bloody-backs because of their red uniforms. Older boys hid behind barns and threw snowballs.

*Paul made this woodcut to show the landing of British soldiers in Boston. The soldiers arrived on ships.*

On March 5, 1770, the teasing went too far. Soldiers clashed with an angry crowd on King Street. There were shoves, shouts, and threats on both sides. Suddenly, the soldiers started firing into the crowd. Five men were killed.

Paul printed an engraving of this "Boston Massacre." The engraving made the townspeople look innocent and the soldiers seem cruel and unfair. That was what Paul wanted. The engraving became his most famous one.

*Paul's engraving of the Boston Massacre made many colonists angry with the British. And that's just what Paul wanted.*

In the spring of 1773, Paul suffered a great loss. His wife, Sarah, died. Thirty-eight-year-old Paul was left to care for the children. One evening, a neighbor named Rachel Walker offered to help. Paul fell in love with the kind and cheerful young woman. Paul and Rachel married that fall and had eight little lambs of their own.

Just a month after Paul and Rachel's wedding, Britain started making more trouble for the colonies. Parliament had ended most of the taxes, but not the tax on tea. It decided that the colonists would have to buy their tea from one British company. The colonists hated this Tea Act most of all.

*Colonists hated the Tea Act. But they still loved tea—and teapots made by Paul Revere.*

One day, three British ships sailed into Boston Harbor carrying tea. The colonists wanted to make sure the tea stayed on the ships. Twenty-five men, including Paul Revere, stood watch day and night.

On the night of December 16, 1773, Paul and the other Sons of Liberty decided to get rid of the tea for good. All over Boston, husbands and fathers rubbed their faces with chimney soot or black grease. They tied ragged blankets around their shoulders. They were trying to look like Indians, a popular symbol of freedom.

The men made their way to the wharf. They split into three groups, one for each tea ship. Paul led his group on board one of the ships. Working quickly, the men hauled all 342 chests of the hated tea onto the decks. They used axes to tear the chests open. Then they dumped the tea into the harbor below.

An artist drew this illustration of the Boston Tea Party.

When they were done, the other men
went home to shake the tea from their
shoes and get some sleep. Not Paul Revere.
The Sons of Liberty had chosen him to
carry a message to New York and
Philadelphia. He brought the news of the
"Boston Tea Party."

# 3 PAUL REVERE SPREADS THE NEWS!

After the Boston Tea Party, the clip-clop of Paul's horse became a familiar sound in the colonies. The patriots relied on him more and more to carry their messages. Everyone knew that Paul Revere was the fastest and most trusted rider around.

In May 1774, Parliament closed the port of Boston until the town agreed to pay for the lost tea. It also filled the town with soldiers—five thousand of them. Paul carried the news to New York and Philadelphia.

That fall, leaders from each colony met in Philadelphia to decide what to do. The meeting was called the Continental Congress. Members of the congress agreed to stand by the Boston patriots. Their decision only made Parliament angrier.

*As a messenger, Paul often carried important messages to cities hundreds of miles away.*

*Paul drew this illustration for a patriot newspaper. The snake stands for the colonies. The dragon is Britain.*

Back and forth went the argument. Back and forth went Paul Revere carrying letters, messages, and news between Boston and Philadelphia.

Many colonists believed that the disagreement would turn into a fight. Paul wanted to know if the British were getting ready for war. He organized groups of townspeople to spy on the soldiers.

In April 1775, the spies learned that the British were planning a surprise attack on the town of Concord, Massachusetts. The townspeople there had stored supplies of guns and ammunition. British soldiers, called Regulars, planned to take the weapons. There had to be a way to warn people.

Lanterns in Christ Church's tall steeple would warn colonists in Charlestown that the British were coming.

Paul worked out a plan with the Sons of Liberty in Charlestown, across the river from Boston. Even if the soldiers stopped him from getting to Charlestown, he wanted to make sure his message would get there.

Paul would have a friend signal to Charlestown from the tall steeple of Christ Church. The friend would hang one lantern if the Regulars marched out on the main road. He would hang two if they used boats to cross the Charles River. The Charlestown men would watch for the signal and spread the word.

Paul didn't have to wait long to try out his signal. On the night of April 18, the news was all over Boston. The Regulars were being loaded onto boats at the Charles River. Once they crossed the river, they would head for Concord.

The Regulars would pass right through the town of Lexington on their way to Concord. Samuel Adams and John Hancock were staying in Lexington. Joseph Warren sent for Paul. He asked Paul to warn the two patriot leaders that the British were marching straight for them. If Hancock and Adams were captured, they might be killed.

*The British called Samuel Adams the most dangerous man in Massachusetts.*

Paul rushed to Christ Church. His friend was waiting to hang the lanterns. Two, Paul told him. Then Paul hurried home, put on his riding clothes, and rushed to the Charles River. Two men met him there to take him across the river.

A huge warship full of Regulars was guarding the mouth of the river. Somehow Paul and the two men managed to cross the river without getting caught. The Charlestown men had seen his signal. They were waiting for him with a horse.

## A FURRY TALE

A Revere family legend says that Paul's little dog followed him to the Charles River. Good thing! At the river, Paul realized he had forgotten his riding spurs. He tied a note for Rachel to the dog's collar. Then he told the dog to go home. In a few minutes, the dog was back with Paul's spurs.

# PAUL REVERE'S RIDE

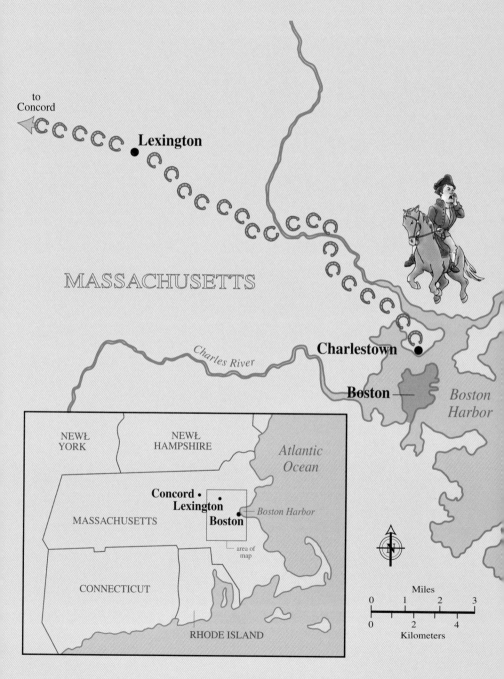

to
Concord

Lexington

MASSACHUSETTS

Charles River

Charlestown

Boston

Boston
Harbor

NEW
YORK

NEW
HAMPSHIRE

Atlantic
Ocean

Concord

Lexington

MASSACHUSETTS

Boston

Boston Harbor

area of
map

CONNECTICUT

RHODE ISLAND

N

Miles

0       1       2       3

0         2         4

Kilometers

*A minuteman barely had time to say good-bye to his family before going off to fight.*

At once, Paul rode off down the moonlit road toward Lexington. At each farmhouse along the way, he paused just long enough to raise the alarm: "The Regulars are out! The Regulars are out!"

In one town, he woke up the captain of the minutemen. These were American soldiers who were ready to battle on a minute's notice. All across the countryside, men grabbed their guns and prepared to fight the Regulars.

Around midnight, Paul arrived in Lexington. He went to the house where Samuel Adams and John Hancock were staying. Of course, they were asleep. A guard outside scolded Paul for making too much noise.

"Noise!" shouted Paul. "You'll have noise enough before long! The Regulars are out!" Then he banged on the door.

John Hancock popped his head out of a window. He recognized Paul. "Come in, Revere," he called out. "We are not afraid of *you*."

When John Hancock heard Paul's news, he got his gun and prepared to join the minutemen. Samuel Adams convinced him to run for his life instead.

Suddenly the whole house was awake. Everyone wanted to hear Paul's news. Another man, William Dawes, arrived at the house just after Paul. He carried the same message Paul did.

Paul had done his job well. But someone still had to ride to Concord and warn the people there. Who better than Paul Revere?

# 4 THE ROAD TO CONCORD

**P**aul and William Dawes got back on their horses and headed for Concord. On the way, they were joined by Samuel Prescott. He was a member of the Sons of Liberty from Concord. The three men stopped only to bang on more doors and awaken more people.

The three had gotten about halfway to Concord. Suddenly Paul spotted a group of British officers on the road ahead. The officers rode up to Paul and pointed their pistols at him. "Stop!" one of them ordered. "If you go an inch further, you are a dead man!"

The officers ordered the men into a pasture by the side of the road. No sooner had they entered the pasture than Samuel Prescott jumped his horse over a stone wall and escaped. William Dawes got away, too. Only Paul was left. His horse was too tired to jump.

*Few people remember the midnight ride of William Dawes. But he was just as brave as Paul Revere.*

Both British soldiers and minutemen carried muskets to defend themselves. But Paul had no weapon when the British captured him.

The officers surrounded Paul. Where had he come from, one of them asked. When had he left? Paul told him. The officer seemed surprised that he had come so far so fast. Then he asked Paul his name. "My name is Revere," Paul replied.

The officer was astonished. "What, Paul Revere?" he said. Even the enemy knew the name of the famous messenger!

Another officer rode up to question Paul. This one pointed a pistol at Paul's head. If Paul did not tell the truth, he would shoot. Paul's voice was calm as he answered. He was a man of truth, he said. And he was not afraid.

## SPREADING THE ALARM

Paul's warning had spread like wildfire. Some of the people he woke up got on their horses, too. They rode to other towns and woke up more people. And those people rode to still more towns and woke up still more people. By the time the Regulars showed up in Lexington, about seventy minutemen were waiting.

The soldiers marched Paul back toward Lexington. As they neared the town, they heard the sound of gunshots. The officers seemed worried. "What was that for?" one asked. Paul told them it was to warn the countryside that the Regulars were coming.

The soldiers weren't sure whether to believe Paul. But if there was going to be a battle, they didn't want him along. They took his horse and let him go.

Paul made his way back to Lexington on foot. He arrived just as Samuel Adams and John Hancock were preparing to leave.

Suddenly Hancock remembered a trunk that he had left behind at a tavern. The trunk was stuffed with the secret papers of the Sons of Liberty. Such a thing must not fall into enemy hands!

Paul and another man headed to the tavern to fetch the trunk. In the pale light of morning they saw fifty or sixty minutemen gathered in the center of the town.

Paul found Mr. Hancock's trunk in an upstairs room of the tavern. Now he and the other man had to carry it away.

*John Hancock's forgotten trunk*

As Paul picked up his end of the trunk, he happened to look out the window. Coming down the road was a sea of red coats and brass buttons. The Regulars had arrived.

Paul and the other man had to hurry back with the trunk. As they went, they passed through the lines of minutemen. From behind, Paul heard a shot, then two. He turned, but he could not see who had fired. Then the morning seemed to explode in a roar of gunfire.

They were the first shots of the American Revolution.

# 5 UNITED STATES OF AMERICA

**P**aul was as busy as ever during the Revolutionary War. When no one wanted to use the old British money, he designed and printed new money. He helped set up a gunpowder mill. And he was still the patriots' favorite messenger.

THIRTY-SIX-SHILLINGS.

Issued in defence of American Liberty

Ense petit placidam sub Libertate Quietem

MAGNA CHARTA

Decmr 7. 1775.

Paul became a lieutenant colonel in the Massachusetts militia. He was in charge of the fort at Castle Island, in Boston Harbor. His work was not very exciting. Mostly, Paul called to passing ships and supervised other soldiers.

The Americans fought the British for eight years. It wasn't until September 3, 1783, that the war officially ended. On that day, Britain and America signed a peace treaty. It said that the United States of America was an independent nation.

Paul settled back into his life as a silversmith. As an American, Paul wanted to sell things made in America. And he wanted to be the one to make them. He already knew how to make beautiful things out of silver and gold. Now he wanted to make practical things out of copper and iron. But first, he had to learn about the science of making metal.

For Paul, learning something new was part of the fun. So he studied books and wrote to experts in chemistry. He learned to make things like anvils and stoves.

## MR. REVERE, DETECTIVE

Sadly, Paul's friend Joseph Warren was killed in the Revolutionary War. The British soldier who buried him stuffed him into a pit with another dead man. By the time the Americans found him, there was not much left of poor Joseph Warren. Only Paul Revere was able to identify the body—by the false teeth he had made for his friend.

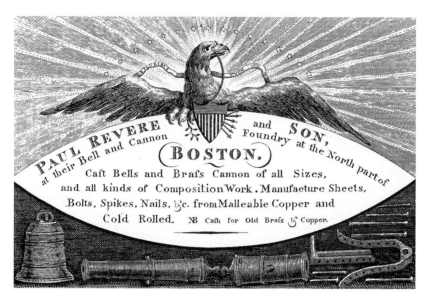

*After the war, Paul and his son went into business together. They made everything from cannons to nails.*

When a church needed a new bell, Paul said he could make that, too. Most people wrinkled their noses when they heard the flat sound of Paul's first bell. He was proud of it just the same. He inscribed it: "The first bell cast in Boston 1792 P. Revere."

Over time, Paul learned to make sweet-sounding bells. Soon people all over New England were called to church by his bells.

Paul was especially proud of his copper work. By 1801, the country was building a navy, and Paul was able to help.

Paul supplied the copper nails, bolts, and spikes the new ships needed. At sixty-six, he was the only man in America who could make the sheets of copper that protected the bottoms of ships.

Paul Revere died on May 10, 1818, after a long and very busy life. He was eighty-three. His silver can be seen in museums. Some of his bells still ring in New England towns. But it is his exciting ride and his fight for freedom that made him famous.

# TIMELINE

PAUL REVERE WAS
PROBABLY BORN ON
DECEMBER 31, 1734

## *In the year . . .*

1748    Paul went to work in his father's shop.    Age 13

1754    his father died.

1756    he fought in the French and Indian War.

1757    he married Sarah Orne.

1758    the first of his sixteen children was born.    Age 23

1765    Parliament passed the Stamp Act.
the Sons of Liberty was formed.

1768    Great Britain sent soldiers to Boston.

1770    the Boston Massacre took place on March 5.    Age 35

1773    his first wife, Sarah, died.
Parliament passed the Tea Act.
he married Rachel Walker.
the Boston Tea Party took place on
December 16.

1774    he was chosen as an express rider for the
1774 Continental Congress.

1775    he made his famous ride to Lexington on    Age 40
April 18.
the first battles of the Revolutionary War
were fought at Lexington and Concord on
April 19.

1783    the Revolutionary War ended on    Age 48
September 3.

1788    he opened an ironware foundry.

1792    he began casting church bells.

1818    he died on May 10.    Age 83

# Two Midnight Rides

Some people think that Henry Wadsworth Longfellow's famous poem is one of the reasons that Paul Revere's ride is remembered and William Dawes's ride is not. Longfellow wrote his poem in 1860. Nearly forty years later, Helen F. Moore wrote a funny poem for Dawes. The first verse of each poem tells a very different story of the midnight ride.

## Paul Revere's Ride
### by Henry Wadsworth Longfellow

Listen, my children, and you shall hear
Of the midnight ride of Paul Revere,
On the eighteenth of April, in Seventy-five;
Hardly a man is now alive
Who remembers that famous day and year.

## The Midnight Ride of William Dawes
### by Helen F. Moore

'Tis all very well for the children to hear
Of the midnight ride of Paul Revere;
But why should my name be quite forgot,
Who rode as boldly and well, God wot?
Why should I ask? The reason is clear —
My name was Dawes and his Revere.

# FURTHER READING

NONFICTION

Edwards, Pamela Duncan. *The Boston Tea Party.* East Rutherford, NJ: Penguin Putnam, 2001. A rhythmic retelling of this pivotal event in colonial history, accompanied by illustrations.

Fritz, Jean. *Why Don't You Get a Horse, Sam Adams?* East Rutherford, NJ: Penguin Putnam, 1996. A lively illustrated biography about the passionate patriot Samuel Adams.

Fritz, Jean. *Will You Sign Here, John Hancock?* East Rutherford, NJ: Penguin Putnam, 1997. A humorous account of the life of John Hancock, with illustrations.

January, Brendan. *The Revolutionary War.* Danbury, CT: New York: Children's Press, 2000. A photo-illustrated overview of the American Revolution.

Moore, Kay. *If You Lived at the Time of the American Revolution.* New York: Scholastic, 1998. Answers questions about what life was like, especially for children, during the Revolutionary War.

FICTION

Lawson, Robert. *Mr. Revere and I.* Boston: Little Brown & Co., 1988. A novel about Paul Revere from the point of view of his very dignified horse.

Longfellow, Henry Wadsworth. *The Midnight Ride of Paul Revere.* Washington, D.C.: National Geographic Publishing, 2000. Wadsworth's poem is paired with mood-setting illustrations by Jeffrey Thompson.

# WEBSITES

**The American Revolution for Kids**
<artemis.simmons.edu/~williamf/AmRev> A good place to start for information about the Revolutionary War, with links to biographies, events, games, interesting facts, maps, a timeline, and further reading.

**The Paul Revere House**
<www.paulreverehouse.org> This museum's website has a "just for kids" link and contains comprehensive information about Paul Revere's life and legacy.

# SELECT BIBLIOGRAPHY

Epstein, Sam, and Beryl Epstein. *Young Paul Revere's Boston.* Champaign, IL: Garrard Publishing Company, 1966.

Fischer, David Hackett. *Paul Revere's Ride.* New York: Oxford University Press, 1994.

Goss, Elbridge Henry. *The Life of Colonel Paul Revere.* Boston: Gregg Press, 1972.

Milton, Joyce. *Paul Revere: Messenger of Liberty.* New York: Bantam Doubleday Dell Publishing Group, Inc., 1990.

Revere, Paul. *Paul Revere's True Accounts of His Famous Ride.* Boston: Massachusetts Historical Society, 1976.

Triber, Jayne E. *A True Republican: The Life of Paul Revere.* Amherst: University of Massachusetts, 1998.

# INDEX

## Acknowledgments

**For photographs and artwork:** © North Wind Archives, pp. 4, 9, 15, 18, 21, 24, 26, 27, 30, 31; © Giraudon/Art Resource, NY, p. 7; Brown Brothers, pp. 8, 17, 20; Boston Museum of Fine Arts, p. 10; American Antiquarian Society, pp. 14, 16, 25, 40, 42; © Hulton/Archive by Getty Collection, p. 35; From the collections of Worcester Historical Museum, Worcester, MA, p. 37. Front and back cover © North Wind Archives.

**For quoted material:** The dialogue that appears on pages 30, 31, 34, 35, and 36 is taken from Paul Revere's own description of his famous ride, as recorded in about 1775.